SPIRITUAL DISCERNMENT

Stephen Kaung

ISBN: 978-1-942521-18-1

Available from:

Christian Testimony Ministry
4424 Huguenot Road
Richmond, Virginia 23235

www.christiantestimonyministry.com

Printed in USA

CONTENTS

WHAT IS SPIRITUAL DISCERMENT?

I Corinthians 2:14-15—But the natural man does not receive the things of the Spirit of God, for they are folly to him; and he cannot know them because they are spiritually discerned; but the spiritual discerns all things, and he is discerned of no one.

Philippians 1:9-11—And this I pray, that your love may abound yet more and more in full knowledge and all intelligence, that ye may judge of and approve the things that are more excellent, in order that ye may be pure and without offence for Christ's day, being complete as regards the fruit of righteousness, which is by Jesus Christ, to God's glory and praise.

Let's have a word of prayer:

Dear Lord, we want to thank Thee for gathering us together unto Thy name. We want to thank Thee for Thy precious promise: "Where two or three are gathered together unto My name there am I in the midst of them." We thank Thee for Thy presence with us. Lord, we pray that Thou will create within us a clean heart, an open mind, and a right spirit. We just pray, Lord, that when Thy word is given Thy Holy Spirit will quicken Thy word to our hearts. Thy word is life and spirit and we believe it. We pray that Thy word will do its work in each one of us. We thank Thee for promising us that if anyone lacks wisdom let him ask and doubt not and Thou will give it to us. So Lord, we do come and confess that we need wisdom. Give to us according to Thy promise. We ask in Thy precious name. Amen.

Thank God for gathering us together again this year. I really feel that every time we meet together it is the tremendous mercy of God. As we are approaching the end, such gatherings become more and more precious. Thank God, He still wants to speak to us; He still wants to bless us.

The theme for this conference is *Spiritual Discernment.* I think everybody knows how we need spiritual discernment, especially in our days. We do look to the Lord that He will give us such discernment that we may be able to live a life that will be pleasing to Him.

In Philippians we find that the apostle Paul prayed for the Philippian believers. As you know, the church in Philippi is noted for its love. In the book of Acts, chapter 16, God led Paul and his companions to Macedonia, to Philippi, and there they found a woman from Thyatira. She listened to the message of the gospel of Jesus Christ and she was touched. She believed in the Lord Jesus, and her whole household. Then she said to Paul and his companions: "If you believe that I am faithful to the Lord, then come and live in my house." She constrained them to live in her house. As soon as she believed in the Lord Jesus, the love of God filled her heart and she expressed that love in a practical way.

Then you remember how a woman with an evil spirit was delivered and because of that, Paul and Silas were imprisoned. While they were in prison in the middle of the night they were praying, singing unto the Lord, praising the Lord, and there was an earthquake. All the gates of the prison were opened, but nobody moved. The jailer thought all the prisoners had escaped. He tried to kill himself but Paul said, "No, we are all here."

Then he said, "What shall I do that I may be saved?"

And Paul said, "Believe in the Lord Jesus and you shall be saved, you and your household."

The jailer and his household believed in the Lord Jesus. He took Paul and Silas to his home, washed them, and fed them.

Paul and Silas were ordered to leave Philippi but they left one man behind, the beloved physician, Luke. So Luke stayed with the Philippian believers. Under his loving care the church in Philippi was noted for its love, and they expressed their love in very practical ways.

PAUL'S PRAYER FOR THE CHURCH IN PHILIPPI

After many years, the apostle Paul was in prison in Rome, and the church in Philippi sent their love to him. In writing back to them, he prayed for them. Now this is the prayer that we all need, not only to hear but to pray: "And this I pray, that your love may abound yet more and more in full knowledge and all spiritual discernment."

In I Timothy 1:5 the apostle Paul said, "The end of what is enjoined [the end of what is being instructed and taught] is love out of a pure heart and a good conscience and unfeigned faith."

Love is the end of all things. God is love. "God so loved the world that He gave His only begotten Son that whosoever believeth in Him shall not perish but have everlasting life." The first and foremost commandment is: "Love thy God with all thy heart, with all thy mind, with all thy strength." Next to it is:"Love one another;ove thy neighbor as thyself." Also we are told in the book of Romans that love sums up all the commandments of God. We should not owe anybody anything but in love we are always in debt. That is the importance of love.

LOVE ABOUNDING

The apostle Paul knew that the Philippian believers had love, yet his prayer for them was that their love might abound more and more. Anything that is living continues to grow. The moment it stops growing, death comes in. Now love is living. It is life and because of this, love must grow. We cannot be satisfied with the little love that we think we have. The moment we are satisfied with our love, spiritual death comes in. Love is something that grows and grows and grows.

Love must abound more and more. But it must abound not only in measure and in depth, it must abound in every area: in judgment, in understanding, and in knowledge. If love is not directed by knowledge, is not governed by discernment, it will be very shallow and it can be misdirected. Sometimes we think love is blind, but love is not blind. Love must abound in full knowledge and all spiritual discernment.

LOVE IN FULL KNOWLEDGE

When we talk about knowledge, we think that knowledge and love are opposites. We can quote I Corinthians 8:2: "Knowledge puffs up; love builds up." Here we find knowledge is something opposite to love. It is because the knowledge there is mental knowledge, something we know in our minds. Even if it is Scriptural knowledge, good knowledge, if it is only mental knowledge it puffs us up. Isn't it true? The more we think we know the Bible, the more we think we are knowledgeable in the Scripture, doesn't that give us a little bit of pride? We think we are more knowledgeable than anybody else. Therefore we are always in the right and other people are always wrong. Knowledge puffs up but only love builds up. A little knowledge is very dangerous.

But what Paul prayed for the saints in Philippi was that their love may abound more and more in full knowledge, real knowledge. Now what is full knowledge, *epignosis?* What is the difference between full knowledge and knowledge as such? Full knowledge in the

Scripture is the knowledge of the eternal will of God. We know God in such a way that we know what His mind is, what His will is, what He desires. That is full knowledge. If you have such full knowledge it will help you in your Christian life because you know where to go, what to choose. Full knowledge in the Scripture is not mental knowledge. It is heart knowledge; it is an experiential knowledge, something that you can experience in your life, something you know in your heart. That is the difference.

Furthermore, full knowledge is practical. Oftentimes we think anything that is spiritual is not practical. If it is practical it is not spiritual; therefore you find people want to be spiritual and become very impractical. But actually, if it is spiritual it is highly practical. It can be practiced, it is practiced, and it will be manifested in words and in deeds. So this is full knowledge.

Love needs to abound more and more in full knowledge. With such knowledge, love knows where to go. Otherwise, you may love that which you should not love. Otherwise, it is just a matter of tolerating everything, thinking that you love because you allow anything, even tolerating sin. You consider that to be love because it has no boundary, no direction. But with full knowledge you know where your love should be applied and should increase.

"All intelligence [all spiritual discernment]." Now this word has been translated in many different ways. In some versions you have "judgment," as in King James: "In all judgment." Some versions say "understanding." Some versions say "insight." Some versions say "perception." And some versions say "spiritual discernment."

What is "all understanding?" What is "spiritual discernment?" Spiritual discernment is not a natural endowment. Some people are born with sharper, keener perception, but that is not what the Scripture is speaking of. Spiritual discernment is not deep in worldly knowledge. Now in Chinese we have a saying: "If you are very deep in earthly affairs, then your heavenly discernment disappears." If you are very deep in earthly affairs, if you know human nature, if you are very observant, and you have lots of experience with the world, your intuitive power begins to disappear because it is all rational and not intuitional. So spiritual discernment is not deep in world affairs.

Spiritual discernment is not psychic; not mind reading. Now some people may develop a kind of psychic power. You know our soul has lots of power. Think of Adam. After God created Adam, He led all the animals before him. Without going to any school, Adam looked at them and named them. Now that is tremendous! He was a natural botanist, a natural person. Such power!

Our soul has tremendous power, but because of sin it is out from under the control of the Spirit of God. Therefore, it is not God's will for us to develop our soul power. We need to develop spirit power, and yet the enemy is trying very hard to develop soul power. Psychic power is everywhere. Spiritual discernment is not psychic power; it is not mind reading. No, spiritual discernment is the opposite of any kind of information or knowledge that comes from the enemy, the devil.

PROVING THE THINGS MORE EXCELLENT

What is spiritual discernment? Spiritual discernment is the ability to discern things that are different and to see through all appearances. Sometimes things may look alike in appearance and it is very confusing. But spiritual discernment is the ability in a confused situation where everything seems to be mixed up, to look through all the darkness and come to a right conclusion, to make the right moral or spiritual choice. That is spiritual discernment.

Spiritual discernment is the power to discern between the true and the false. It is the power to discern between that which is of the spirit and that which is of the soul. Spiritual discernment is the ability to distinguish between that which is of the flesh and that which is of the spirit. Spiritual discernment is the ability to discern all things spiritual. Spiritual discernment is the ability to discern what is in man, not by judging the outward appearance but by touching the spirit that is in man. Spiritual discernment is the ability to discern what is the will of God and what is not His will. Not only that, it is also the ability to make the right and proper moral and spiritual choice. Now that is spiritual discernment.

Isn't this something that we are greatly lacking? How often we are surrounded by situations where we find it very difficult to know what is right, what is wrong, what is of God, what is of man, what is of the spirit and what is of the soul, what is myself and what is of God. Oftentimes we are confused; we are puzzled. As a matter of fact, in our daily life we are faced with such situations all the time. Under that kind of situation how important it is that we have spiritual discernment!

Spiritual discernment is in the spirit. It is not trying to discern by what you hear or by what you see—by the visible. But spiritual discernment is to see, to hear in your spirit; it is by the illumination of the Holy Spirit. This is a spiritual functioning, a spiritual exercise that is most necessary in our days.

Paul's prayer for the Philippian believers was that their love might abound more and more in full knowledge and all spiritual discernment. In other words, this spiritual discernment is an all around one, a total one. Sometimes we may have some discernment in a certain area but in another area we are completely blind. What we need is an all around spiritual discernment. With that kind of spiritual discernment then we are able to walk rightly before God. Without it, how can we walk pleasing to our God?

We need to pray that our love may abound more and more in full knowledge and all spiritual discernment. With this spiritual discernment then we will be able to judge and approve the things that are more excellent.

F. B. Meyer has a very good explanation of this spiritual discernment. He said the word *understanding* (some versions use the word understanding) is a word that is used many times in the book of Proverbs. And in the book of Isaiah, chapter 11, it says, "The Spirit of the Lord is the Spirit of wisdom and understanding." Now the understanding there is quick understanding; it is a quickening of scent. He said if someone is in deep love he or she will be very quick in detecting anything that may hurt or offend the one whom he or she loves. Isn't that true? If you are not in love you may hurt and offend people without sensing anything. But if you really love a person, you sense it when even a gesture, a slight movement, a facial expression may hurt and offend the one whom you love. You know it. So he said: One who is in love with God will sense in his life, in his habit, in his behavior, in his way of life, any small thing, any slight deviation that may hurt the God whom he loves.

The power of smelling is mysterious. You cannot explain it. Even before you see anything, hear any voice, you already can smell something, and that is spiritual discernment. You have a quick sense of that kind of scent in you. With spiritual discernment, love can go in the right way. Otherwise, you may love what should not be loved.

JUDGING THINGS THAT DIFFER

"In order that you may judge of and approve the things that differ." With that kind of full knowledge and spiritual discernment, then you can judge things, you can understand, you can distinguish. Not only that, you can prove and even approve of the things that differ.

"The things that differ" is put in different ways in different versions because in the original it contains both ideas. In some versions it says, "the things that differ." It is the same word that you find in I Corinthians 15: "The glory of one star differs from the glory of another star." Some versions put it "excellent" like in Matthew 6, where our Lord Jesus said, "You are more excellent than the lily that God has so cared for and given such glory." You are more excellent.

So whether it is the things that differ or the things that are more excellent, you find that things are not the same. Things are different. There are things that are more excellent, and it is the will of God that we should not be bogged down with things that are just okay. He wants us to aim at the excellent. And it is only if you have that full knowledge and spiritual discernment that your love can choose the things that are really different and the things that are more excellent.

Do you know that we as believers are not supposed to be ordinary? We are supposed to be extraordinary. Now that is what you find in the Sermon on the Mount. The Lord said that if you just greet those whom you love, well, the world does the same. You are just ordinary. But if we can love our enemies, that is extraordinary. God wants us to be extraordinary. How can we be extraordinary unless we know how to direct our love to choose the things that differ, the things that are more excellent.

SPIRITUAL DECEPTION IS EVERYWHERE

Spiritual discernment is very, very important to our spiritual life. Without spiritual discernment our spiritual life will be all in a mess. Do we really see the need of it? Do we really desire for it? We are living in a world that is very dangerous. Even at the time of Peter, Paul, and John in the first century, in II Peter he mentioned that there were already many false teachers and false prophets who were even denying the Master who bought them with such a price.

We are living in such a world. In II Timothy, Paul said that this is a perilous time because people have become lovers of self, lovers of money, lovers of pleasure, instead of lovers of God and lovers of good." Now remember, he is talking not only of the world as such; he is even talking about the religious world, the so-called Christian world. People become lovers of self, lovers of money, lovers of pleasure, and they are not lovers of God. We are supposed to be lovers of God, in love with God, and lovers of good, but that is the world we are living in. In I John, the apostle John said, "Little children, you have heard that the antichrist will come, but the spirit of antichrist is already here."

We are living in a very dangerous world. This world is temporarily under the usurpation of the devil. Satan is called the prince of this world, and in the book of Revelation, chapter 12, you will find that this dragon, this old serpent deceives the whole world. Satan is a liar. There is no truth in him, our Lord Jesus said. He is a liar and he deceives the whole world. He made the whole world just a big lie. Deception is everywhere. People live in this big lie, under this big deception, and yet they think they are wise, they are clever, they are right, they are going the right way. Deception is one of the strongest tactics of the enemy. Do not think that you can never be deceived. If you think you can never be deceived, you are already deceived. We are living in such a world.

Even in the so-called spiritual world you find the war between spiritual discernment and spiritual deception is going on all the time. Not only that, but the principle of the world we are living in is relativity. Everything is relative. There is no absolute standard. Everything is gray. You cannot know whether it is white or black because it is gray. And how easily we are deceived when we are under such circumstances. We make wrong right, right wrong, true false, false true. That is the reason why we need spiritual discernment. Thank God, in James it says, "If anyone lacks wisdom, let him ask God who is wisdom and He will give, but doubt not." This is what we need.

Spiritual discernment is not only necessary because we are surrounded by liars, by deception, by the enemy, and the world, but spiritual discernment is also necessary because of something positive. It is not all negative. So the apostle Paul's prayer for the Philippian believers was that their love may abound more and more in full knowledge and all spiritual discernment in order that they may judge of and approve of the things that are more excellent in order that they may be pure.

LIVING TRANSPARENT LIVES

Brothers and sisters, as believers we must not only be delivered from all these lies and deceptions that are around us, but it is the will of God that we may live pure on this earth. Now what does the word *pure* really mean? We are told that the word itself carries the meaning of bringing something, maybe a garment or something, to the light of the sun. You put it under the sunlight so you can see whether it is stained or soiled or whether it is clean, because in the darkness you do not know whether there are any spots there. But if you put it under the sunlight then everything is clear. Therefore the word *pure* means "spotless." Under the sunlight

19

it appears to be without spot, and because of that this word can also be known as transparent. What the Lord desires is that we may be pure, so pure that we are transparent.

Isn't it true that our life is rather opaque? We dare not be transparent. There are things in our lives that have to be hidden. We will not allow people to look through us. Transparency is dangerous because where can we hide? But God's will is that we may be transparent—all the opaqueness, all the darkness, all the hidden things of life rejected. It is just like the apostle Paul said in II Corinthians 4:2: "We have rejected the hidden things of shame, not walking in deceit, nor falsifying the word of God, but by manifestation of the truth commending ourselves to every conscience of men before God." How he denied all the things that would affect the testimony of God, that he might be presented to every conscience. God's desire is that we be transparent, and if you are transparent, anything that appears before you will be discerned in its right color. That is spiritual discernment.

The reason we are lacking in spiritual discernment is because we are not transparent. God's will is that we may be pure, transparent, spotless, and without offence. In some versions it says, "blameless, without blemish." But actually the word in itself means that you do not cause anyone to be offended nor are you offended by anything. That is the meaning of it.

In one sense, in this world it is almost impossible that there will be no offence. Sometimes we become the stone of offence; sometimes we are offended by other people. But if you have spiritual discernment you will not be a cause of offence to anybody. Oftentimes we offend people without knowing it because we are in darkness. But if we really have spiritual discernment we will not be a cause of offence to anybody. We will not knowingly, deliberately put anything before our brothers and sisters who are blind that they fall over it. Neither will you be offended. Why? Because you know too well to be offended.

Our Lord Jesus said, "Blessed are those who are not offended in Me." What does He mean? It means that sometimes the Lord does something that you do not understand, or you expect Him to do something that He does not do, and you are offended because you are lacking in full knowledge and spiritual discernment. If you really understand the Lord you will not be offended by Him. You know that what He does is best for you even if you do not know how to explain it.

We are living in a world, even among Christians, brothers and sisters, you find offence everywhere. Is there anyone here who has never been not offended? Is there anyone here who has not offended someone? How we need to be delivered that we may live a life without offence! And you can only come to such life if you have spiritual discernment.

THE DAY OF CHRIST

"For the day of Christ." What is the day of Christ? In the Scripture, the day of Christ has a very special meaning. In the New Testament, every time you find the day of Christ, the day of Christ Jesus, Christ's day, you know it points to the day when Christ shall return and we shall all appear before Him at His judgment seat. That is the day of Christ. If you really love the Lord, if you really follow Him, if you live a life pure and without offence, then you will be looking forward to that day. If you read the epistles written by Paul, you find that it is his heart's desire—longing, waiting for that day to come. But if you are not living a life pure and without offence, probably you will be like that evil servant and say the Lord is not coming yet. He delays; He is not coming. You are afraid to see His face.

Now how can we be prepared so that when our Lord Jesus shall return and we all shall appear before His judgment seat, we welcome that day, we look forward to that day? It is because we live as He lived.

Brothers and sisters, how do you live your day every day? Do you live your day as one who thinks you can live to be a hundred years old? Or do you live your days with the light of the day of Christ in view? Are you looking forward to that day when Christ shall return and you shall see

Him? Is it in that light you live every day? How can you do that without spiritual discernment?

BEARING THE FRUIT OF RIGHTEOUSNESS

"Being complete as regards the fruit of righteousness, which is by Jesus Christ." Living such a life, a life of love with full knowledge and all spiritual discernment, you will bear the fruit of righteousness, not by yourself but by Jesus Christ. This fruit of righteousness is your wedding garment. In Revelation 19 the bride has made herself ready and she is clothed with a garment of white, shining linen which is the righteousnesses of the saints. The righteousness of Christ is being constituted, built up within you, so in turn you also bear the fruit of righteousness. That will become your wedding garment, making you fit to attend that wedding feast. And it is all to God's glory and praise.

Brothers and sisters, the ultimate is God's glory and praise. It is not that you may be a spiritual giant. Oh, how we want to be spiritual, that we may be looked up to, put on a pedestal. No; you desire to have such love with knowledge and intelligence and live such a pure life without offence, full of the fruit of righteousness—not for yourself; it is for God. It is for the glory of God and for His praise because after all it is all His grace. You have nothing to boast of. This is spiritual discernment.

ILLUSTRATIONS OF SPIRITUAL DISCERNMENT

I would like to illustrate it. Let's look at our Lord Jesus. When our Lord was on earth, He was a Man full of wisdom, of spiritual discernment. When Andrew led Simon, his brother, to Him, do you know what our Lord did? The Lord looked at him and in the original it means "the Lord looked up and down at him." Did you ever have anyone who looked you up and down? You will tremble, right? The Lord looked him up and down and Simon was speechless. Isn't that strange? That talkative Simon was speechless. Why? The Lord looked through him. He said, "You are Simon, that's what you are, but you shall be Peter. The grace of God can transform you into a stone, a living stone to be built into the house of God." That is spiritual discernment.

Nathaniel. The Lord looked at Nathaniel and said, "You are a true Israelite. Nathaniel said, "How did You know me?" (because he was an Israelite). The Lord said, "Before Philip called you, I saw you under the fig tree." You know, the fig tree symbolized the nation of Israel. Nathaniel was thinking about Israel—a true Israelite—but the Lord saw through. So he said, "My Lord and my God." And the Lord said, "You shall see greater things than these. You shall see the angels of God ascending and descending on the Son of Man."

When our Lord did miracles, many believed in Him. But when you come to the end of John 2, you find the Lord did not commit Himself to them because He knew what was in man. That is spiritual discernment.

Nicodemus came with very courteous, flattering words. The Lord pointed at him and said, "You must be born again." There is no need to pretend. How the Pharisees and the scribes put on a form of godliness! But the Lord looked through them and said, "You hypocrites, woe to you."

Peter confessed the Lord and yet he held on to the Lord and said, "Lord, You will never go to the cross." The Lord was not deceived by this self-love. The Lord said, "Satan, get behind me because you are not mindful of God, but mindful of man." Think of that. Why is it that our Lord had such discernment? Before the disciples asked Him anything, He already knew what they were talking about behind Him. Is He a mind reader? No; He is so transparent that the reality is wide open on everything that comes in His presence,. Nothing can be hidden from Him because all things are naked before God. That is spiritual discernment. But how that discernment is exercised with humility and with love!

Peter denied the Lord three times. Nevertheless, by the sea, in that morning the Lord said, "Simon, son of Jonah, do you love Me more than these?" Simon Peter knew his weakness. He dared not boast anymore. He said, "Lord, You know I have good feelings about You." The Lord said, "Feed My lambs." Such love! Such humility!

We see it even in the way our Lord treated Judas. He knew Judas was a betrayer from the very beginning, and yet He treated him in such an honorable way. He knew he was a thief, but He gave him the bag. Even at the last Passover supper when He said one of them was going to betray Him, John who was lying on the bosom of the Lord said, "Who is he?" The Lord said, "The one to whom I give this bread that is dipped in the sauce is he." According to custom this was an act of honoring the honorable guest. So the Lord used a symbol that is entirely opposite to what it is so that the disciples never sensed it, never knew. When Judas went out, they thought the Lord wanted him to buy something or give something to the poor. It was discernment exercised with love. That is what we need.

The apostles, because of their life with the Lord, also had their spiritual discernment sharpened. In Acts 3, John and Peter went to the temple to pray and a man lame from birth was asking for alms. Peter and John looked at him and saw there was faith in him. That is spiritual discernment.

Ananias and Sapphira tried to cheat the Holy Spirit. Peter knew at once. Simon, the magician tried to buy the gift of God, the Holy Spirit. Peter saw through him: "You are in the gall of bitterness."

The same thing happened to Paul in Acts, chapter 13. Paul was in Paphos, and Elymas, a magician, tried to resist, and Paul could see how he was bound by the adversary.

Brothers and sisters, spiritual discernment is the need of our time. I lay this matter before you. Take it up very seriously. Go to the Lord. Ask for spiritual discernment. I desperately need it. We all desperately need it And the Lord is ready to give to us. Ask and it shall be given.

Shall we pray:

Dear Lord, Thou art all wisdom and all spiritual discernment. Lord, Thou art the source of spiritual discernment. We come to Thee and humble ourselves before Thee, acknowledging that we are lacking, greatly lacking in spiritual discernment—almost nothing. Oh, have mercy upon us. Lord, give to Thy people, in these perilous days, spiritual discernment that we may be able to be delivered from all deceptions and confusions and be able to walk pure, spotless, transparent, and righteous before Thee. Lord, have mercy upon us. We ask in Thy precious name. Amen.

ATTAINING SPIRITUAL DISCERNMENT

I Corinthians 2:14-15—But the natural man does not receive the things of the Spirit of God, for they are folly to him; and he cannot know them because they are spiritually discerned; but the spiritual discerns all things, and he is discerned of no one.

Philippians 1:9-11—And this I pray, that your love may abound yet more and more in full knowledge and all intelligence [or all spiritual discernment], that ye may judge of and approve the things that are more excellent, in order that ye may be pure and without offence for Christ's day, being complete as regards the fruit of righteousness, which is by Jesus Christ, to God's glory and praise.

We are fellowshiping on this matter of spiritual discernment. I hope that everyone senses the desperate need for spiritual discernment because we are living in a day of great confusion. We need spiritual discernment that we may be able to distinguish between true and false, right and wrong, spiritual or natural, soulish or spiritual, God's will or man's idea. We live in a world of great deception and we need spiritual discernment to see through the counterfeit, the darkness that is around us. Spiritual discernment is necessary for us to live a life that is pleasing to God, that walks in the will of God. So our burden is that in these last, difficult days God will grace us with spiritual discernment.

We mentioned that spiritual discernment is not a natural endowment. We are all made differently. Some people are naturally endowed with more keenness of sense. They seem to be able to see things more clearly, but this is not what is meant by spiritual discernment because spiritual discernment is not something natural.

Spiritual discernment is not the deep knowledge of the world. Some people have lots of worldly experiences, and because of that they seem to have a kind of perception that other people may not have. But this is not what we mean by spiritual discernment. As a matter of fact, the more deeply you are wise and prudent in the world, the less spiritual discernment you have.

You remember what our Lord Jesus said when He was rejected by Capernaum, Chorazin, and the places that He had worked many wonders and spoke many words? He lifted up His eyes to heaven and said, "Father, I thank Thee because this is Thy good pleasure. Thou dost reveal Thyself to the babes but to the wise and prudent Thou dost hide Thyself." It is not worldly wisdom that we are talking about.

Spiritual discernment is not psychic power. Especially in these last days, the enemy is trying to stir up psychic power, but this is not what the Lord wants. Spiritual discernment is something from God, something from the Holy Spirit, a discerning power that we are given deep in our spirit. It is the spiritual ability to distinguish between the good and evil, to distinguish between true and false, to distinguish between flesh and spirit, between self and God, between what is of God and what is of man. That is spiritual discernment and that is something we need very much in our days.

Now we would like to go a step further and see how we come to this spiritual discernment. If you realize the need of it and furthermore you realize that you do not have it as you should, then it is time to talk about how we can attain this spiritual discernment. But before we do that, I think we would like to clarify one thing.

DISCERNING OF SPIRITS

Spiritual discernment is different from that spiritual gift you find in I Corinthians 12:10. For the sake of the body of Christ, the Holy Spirit manifests Himself in the body in different members of the body by giving them different spiritual gifts. One of the spiritual gifts is the discerning of spirits. Discerning of spirits is a gift; it is a spiritual gift. It is a manifestation of the Holy Spirit. The Holy Spirit gives such a gift to some members of the body and they are able to discern the spirits. There are many spirits in the unseen world. Not only is there the Spirit of God, not only the good angels, good spirits, but there are many angels who have rebelled against God—evil spirits. So we need to be able to discern whether it is God's Spirit or whether it is an evil spirit.

Satan transforms himself as an angel of light. In other words, the evil spirits sometime try to imitate the Spirit of God and that is why we need the discerning of spirits. This is given especially to some members of the body of Christ. Not all members of the body of Christ have such gift. I thank God that He does not give the same gift to everybody because it shows us how we need one another. No one of us is perfect, complete, has every gift. If you did you would not need your brothers or sisters anymore. But God is after the body, not just an individual. We need one another. That is the reason God gives the discerning of spirits to some members, especially in the time of revivals.

When a revival comes, the Holy Spirit is working in a very prominent way. But when the Holy Spirit is working in such a manner, the evil spirits try to confuse, and they will come in and work very hard. That is why, especially in revivals, when the manifestation of the Spirit is so prominent, you find all kinds of confusion begins to come in. It is the enemy trying to confuse, perplex people.

For instance, during the Welsh Revival (There was a great revival in Wales in 1904-05.) many came to the Lord and the manifestation of the Holy Spirit was clear. But at the same time the enemy came in and tried to imitate, counterfeit, and confuse people. Because of this, later on, Evan Roberts in cooperation with Mrs. Jessie Penn-Lewis, wrote that book called *War on the Saints.* That was the experience that Evan Roberts had during the Welsh Revival. And with the knowledge that Mrs. Penn-Lewis had they wrote a book that delivered many people who were in confusion and even in deception. Especially at a time when the Holy Spirit is very clearly manifested, we need those with the gift of discerning of spirits.

SPIRITUAL DISCERNMENT IS GRACE

Spiritual discernment is different from the discerning of spirits. Why? because the discerning of spirits is a gift, and because it is a gift, the Holy Spirit just gives to some, not to all, according to His will. But spiritual discernment is not a gift; it is grace. Because it is grace, it is for all. That is the difference between gift and grace. Whenever it is a matter of gift you will find that some have, some do not. Some have this gift, some have another gift, but of course every member has at least one gift that we may function in the body of Christ, for the body of Christ. But grace is impartial. Grace is universal. Grace is given to all. Spiritual discernment is a grace not a gift. That is why it is open to all the brothers and sisters, to everyone. It is open to you. It is open to me. It is open to all. That is spiritual discernment.

In a sense, every believer has a measure of spiritual discernment. It comes with life. When you believe in the Lord Jesus, you are born again, born from above. You receive a new life, the life of Christ, God's own life. With that life you

37

receive a certain measure of spiritual discernment. It comes with life. It comes with the quickening of your dead spirit.

We were all created with a spirit, a soul, and a body. With the body we have world consciousness. We are aware of the world around us by our five senses. With the soul we are conscious of our selves because we think, we feel, we decide. With our spirit we should be conscious of God because God is the proper environment of our spirit.

The Lord's word to Adam was: "You shall not eat the tree of the knowledge of good and evil, for on the day that you eat thereof you shall surely die. You will die on that very day, that very moment." But we know Adam lived over nine hundred years, physically speaking, and he begot sons and daughters. Soulically speaking, he was still alive. What was dead? His spirit was dead. Unfortunately, when sin came in, his spirit was dead. Now it does not mean his spirit as a created organ disappeared or was annihilated. It was there, but his spirit was dead to its proper environment. In other words, it had lost its contact with God and that is why before we were saved we lost contact with God. God became an unknown to us. People can communicate with evil spirits but they cannot communicate with God. But thank God, when you believe in the Lord Jesus, you are born again. He that is born of the Spirit is spirit. That which is born of the Holy Spirit is the human spirit. Your spirit was quickened into life, renewed. Not only did you receive a new spirit, your contact with God instantly resumed, calling out, "Abba Father," and the Holy Spirit came and dwelt in your new spirit.

In Ezekiel we are told God said, "I will give you a new spirit and I will put My Spirit into your spirit." We who believe in the Lord Jesus receive a new life, the life of God, the life of Jesus Christ, and at the same time a new spirit with the indwelling of the Holy Spirit. When that happens there is a certain measure of spiritual discernment that dwells in you.

You may not know much about the word of God yet. You may be a new Christian, but there is something in you that gives you a certain amount of spiritual discernment. It is the life in you; it is the Holy Spirit in you. That discernment does not come from outward observation or knowledge; it comes from your spirit.

Several years ago a man got saved. He came from a heathen background and he did not even know the word of God. He was newly saved but soundly saved. He went to Boston where he went to a meeting and heard a message. (Now remember, he was a new Christian and he did not have much knowledge of the Scripture.) As he listened to the preacher, when the preacher said, "We are God-men," something within him said, "No, it cannot be." He could not explain it because he had no Scriptural knowledge but somehow he sensed something was not right. Later on he said, "To call a person "a man of God" is reasonable, but to call a man "God-man" does not sound right. Even though he was a new Christian and had no Scriptural knowledge, there was a certain amount of spiritual discernment in him .

THE ANOINTING DWELLS WITHIN

I John refers to little children, babes in Christ. And in I John 2, the apostle John says to little children, "You are living in the last hour and the spirit of antichrist is everywhere." How are you going to live through such a world? Babes are easily misled. They will be swayed by every wind of doctrine. When people come in with one doctrine, you are blown in that direction. When people come in with another doctrine, you are blown in another direction. Babes are easily swayed because they do not have the right knowledge. But thank God, He has given provision to deliver from deception even for babes in Christ. Why? It is because the anointing dwells in us. The Holy Spirit who dwells in us is the anointing. The anointing means that the ointment is softly, tenderly applied upon some wounds and makes you feel comfortable, right. That is the way the Holy Spirit works in our spirit. He is there as our teacher, our unfailing teacher. He will teach us in all things. Remember these words are spoken to little children. As little children in Christ, the Holy Spirit who dwells in us is teaching us incessantly in

41

everything great and small. Whatever He teaches is true and is not a lie. How can we know this is a lie or this is true? Sometimes a lie looks very much like truth. The Holy Spirit will teach you in great things and in small things, and whatever He teaches is true; it is not a lie. If you obey the teaching of the anointing you abide in Christ.

That is the reason why, even as little children, babes in Christ, God has already given us a provision, a certain amount of spiritual discernment. Of course, being young in spiritual things, you may be mistaken. That is why in the same portion of Scripture the apostle John said, "If you keep what you have heard from the beginning, then you abide in God and you abide in Christ." In other words, because there is the possibility of being mistaken, you really need to go to the word of God, to check with the word of God to see if you find it in the word or if you cannot find it, if it agrees with the word or it is opposite to the word, contrary to the word. Then with the leading of the Spirit within you and with the word of God before you, you are able to discern what is of God and what is not of God.

THE INWARD WAY OF LIFE

Unfortunately, among God's people there is a basic lack. After we are saved we are not being taught of this inward way of life. We are being led away from living an inward way of life, that is, a life lived by listening to the voice of the Holy Spirit. By not having that inward relationship with God, we are led astray to the outward. We are being taught many rules and regulations. We are told that if we want to be a good Christian there are things that we should do and there are things that we should not do. Furthermore, we make many laws and rules and regulations for ourselves. We all have our own standard of living a Christian life, of what a Christian life is, and we make all kind of rules and regulations for ourselves. We bind ourselves with outward laws and rules. Our walk is an outward walk, not an inward way. Because of that, we neglect to hear the still small voice within us. We do not have the habit.

There are spiritual habits we need to cultivate. Just like with our physical life there are certain habits, good habits we need to develop.

As Christians we need to develop certain spiritual habits. If we do not develop these habits then our spiritual senses are dormant, are not being used. So it is very important that at the start of our Christian life we realize what God has given to us—life, a new life.

Spiritual discernment is a matter of life. It is not a matter of outside knowledge. Some people may have great knowledge, but they have little discernment. Spiritual discernment is based on life, the life of Christ in you, as manifested by the Holy Spirit. That is the foundation of spiritual discernment. If you let this new life in you develop and grow, then your spiritual discernment also grows. If you neglect this inner life, then your spiritual discernment will not grow.

THE NATURE OF THE LIFE WITHIN

Every life has its nature. The old Adamic life in us has its nature. What is its nature? It always goes in the direction of sin and rebellion. That is the nature of human life. That is why the first word that a baby knows and says is "no." That is the first indication of Adamic life, a life of rebellion.

To sin is natural; not to sin is unnatural. If you follow that natural life, if you develop according to the nature of that life, there is no reason to be surprised that you live such a corrupted, sinful life because that is its nature. But God has given us a new life. It is God's uncreated life. It is the life of Christ. It has been demonstrated on this earth what kind of life it is—so pure, so holy, so righteous, so loving, so full of light, no darkness at all. This is the nature of this life in you and what you need is to cultivate that life, follow the nature of that life.

When you are faced with a problem, this life within you, the Holy Spirit who dwells in you, will tell you which direction to go. If you go in that direction, you feel peace and life within you. If you go against that direction, you will feel spiritual death in you. I believe we all have such experiences. When we are faced with a problem and we do not know what to do, if we follow our natural life, our natural like and dislike, we will go a certain way. But you find there is another life within you that is clean, holy, separated, that shrinks back from such.

If you persist in following the natural life, what happens? That is the difference between a Christian and a non-Christian. A Christian should not sin, but a Christian can sin. Now suppose you sin, what is the difference between you and a non-Christian? Outwardly, there is no difference. But actually, there is a difference because when a non-Christian sins, there is a pleasure there. He feels comfortable. He feels, in a sense, a false glory. But if a Christian sins, he feels miserable. Why? The new nature in you says, "No, that is against my nature."

Brothers and sisters, as believers, how we need to follow the new nature within us. If you develop that nature it will become a habit, and when habits are formed, a character begins to appear. The personality of Christ is being revealed, manifested in your life. So spiritual discernment is a matter of life. There is no short cut to spiritual discernment. You need to follow life, seek the eternal life, as the Scripture says.

Follow life. You need to exercise your spiritual senses.

EXERCISE THE SPIRIT

In Hebrews 5:14 we are told babies can only drink milk. What is milk? Milk is predigested food. Babies cannot eat meat, they cannot eat solid food, so the mother will eat meat and solid food, and she will digest it. After it is digested, it becomes milk to nourish the babies.

Why is it that babies cannot consume solid food? It is because they are not skillful in it. They have not been exercised. But as a grown-up, you are able to consume solid food because you are skillful. You have exercised your senses; therefore you are able to consume solid food.

Spiritually, this is the same thing. We need exercise. You remember Paul said to Timothy in I Timothy 4:7-8: "Exercise yourself unto godliness." We need to exercise ourselves unto "like God." Physical exercise, exercise of the body has little profit. There is some profit, especially with young people. You need physical exercise. It is profitable. You cannot study all the day; you need to take time out to have some physical exercise. It is good for your body. But physical exercise, its profit is little. All it gives you is a healthy body, and that is just for a short time, your life duration. But spiritual exercise, exercise unto godliness, is profitable, not only in this age but even in the age to come. But do we exercise spiritually?

What is spiritual exercise? In the Roman days, especially with the Greeks, their beauty was bodily beauty. So they sent their children to gymnasiums to develop a well-formed body, to go through all kinds of exercises under a tutor so that they could develop an all-round, beautiful body. But as believers, we need to go into the gymnasium too. Our gymnasium is the world. Your every day life, every day occurrences and events, people you meet, things you face, events that come to you are all instruments in the gymnasium. We are there to exercise our spirit under a tutor, of course. Physically, if you want to do exercise you need an instructor. Otherwise, you may hurt yourself. Spiritually, the same thing is true. For us to have spiritual exercise we need a tutor, an instructor. Thank God He has provided us an instructor—the Holy Spirit. He is our instructor. He knows exactly what we need to develop that spiritual discernment. So He puts us into all kinds of circumstances.

We often say that to a believer there is nothing that happens by chance. God has ordered the details of our life. The Holy Spirit has arranged every circumstance for us. We call it the discipline of the Holy Spirit. He arranges all kinds of circumstances and puts us in there. But there He wants us to exercise our spirit. The more you exercise your spirit the sharper it becomes.

Conscience

We need to exercise our conscience. A Christian conscience is very important. In the world, everybody has a conscience. That is the last trace of the function of the spirit that still remains. Thank God for that, otherwise we would never be saved. God left a little trace of conscience there, so our heart can be pricked, our conscience can be pierced. But to a fallen man the conscience is not the standard because the standard of conscience is God. It is not culture, not history, not custom, not teaching; it is God. The conscience of an unbeliever is not dependable. Even a robber says, "I do everything by my conscience." A cannibal can eat another person and be very proud of it. His conscience never bothers him. But to a believer, the moment you are saved, your conscience of the heart has been cleansed and God has become the standard of your conscience. The Holy Spirit is speaking to you through your conscience. So sometimes we say the conscience is the voice of God. We need to learn to listen to the voice of our conscience.

Oftentimes you find there is a battle there. Your reasoning says "yes," but your conscience says "no." Listen to your conscience. You need to exercise your conscience. When your conscience is pricked, when your conscience is touched, do not quench it, do not neglect it. Listen to it. Pay attention to it. We need to keep a conscience without offense before God and man. That is exercising our spiritual sense. When you exercise your spiritual sense, then your spiritual discernment gets sharper. In whatever area you are being dealt with by God, in that particular area you are very sensitive. Whenever something happens in that area, you discern it immediately, not only in you but also in other people. But in places where you have neglected your conscience, you will be kept in the dark. You will not be able to detect it in yourself or in other people because you have not exercised your conscience to distinguish between good and evil.

Intuition

We need to exercise our intuition; that is the direct knowledge from God. God speaks to us directly, to our spirit. It is not information that we have gathered from outside; it is a direct speaking of God. We need to exercise our intuition.

Communion

We need to exercise our communion power, to commune with the Lord. The more you commune with the Lord, the keener will be your perception. Exercise.

EXERCISE THE SOUL

Brothers and sisters, there is so much we need to learn. All the functions of our spirit need to be exercised. The more you exercise them, the sharper they become. As a matter of fact, not only does our spirit need exercise, but even our soul needs to be exercised. We need to exercise our will to submit to the will of God. We need to exercise our mind to have the mind of Christ. We need to exercise emotion that we may be delivered from the natural emotion and our emotion be the expression of the love of God, of the love of Christ. That is why we need to deny ourselves, take up the cross and follow the Lord. This is exercise in the soulical realm.

EXERCISE THE BODY

We need to exercise spiritually even in the physical realm. You remember Paul said in I Corinthians 9: "I buffet my body and put it underneath me." We will not allow our body to rule over us. The body has its own lusts, has its own passions. We need to control it, put it underneath us. That is not asceticism, ill-treating our body. No; that is disciplining it, so we will not be controlled by the passions of our body, but are able to put it underneath us and become slaves to the righteousness of God. These are exercises.

Christians today are not exercising. We do not even know how to be a Christian, to live a Christian life. We all live outwardly. It is not real. Real Christian living is a life within. Spiritual exercises are going on all the time, led by the Spirit of God, that we might be increasing in the knowledge of God, knowing Him, gaining Christ. And our spiritual discernment is increasing all the time. It comes with life.

THE DANGER OF SPIRITUAL DISCERNMENT

But then, dear brothers and sisters, spiritual discernment is sacred. In spiritual things, on the one hand it is glorious; but on the other hand it is very dangerous. Spiritual discernment is a glorious thing because you are able to discern, know what is right, what is wrong, know God's will and man's opinion, know what is of yourself and what is of God, what is the soul, what is the spirit, the world and God. It is glorious; but it is very dangerous. If spiritual discernment is not exercised with humility, it is the most dangerous thing. Spiritual discernment has to be accompanied by humility. As a matter of fact spiritual discernment is self-knowledge. You know yourself. You cannot know God if you do not know yourself, but you will not be able to know yourself by yourself. Our heart is deceitful above all things. Self-knowledge comes through dealings, through discipline, through exercises, through the growth of life. As you grow in the Lord, you know more of yourself. You know more how miserable you are, how wicked you are, that there is nothing good in yourself. It gives you this knowledge, and with this knowledge you know God—how good, how perfect, how glorious He is.

Unfortunately, if spiritual discernment is developed to a certain point, when you begin to be proud of your spiritual discernment because you can see what others do not see, and pride begins to come into your life, that is the downfall. You enter into deception and that deception is the darkest of all deceptions. You become proud. You become critical. You become hard and you are totally deceived. You think you are always right. You think you always see the right thing and because you see you cannot bear other people. This is the risk, the danger of spiritual discernment.

Therefore, spiritual discernment has to be accompanied with humility. As a matter of fact, it should humble you because if you can discern, you see how bad you are, how wicked you are, how nothing you are. It is all of God's grace that you can even exist. Everything is grace, grace, grace. It should humble you. It should not elate you, but unfortunately, that is what we are, and we fall into deep deception.

So dear brothers and sisters, there is a warning here. Spiritual discernment is not for boasting; it is not for criticizing. It is for your spiritual maturity and it is for your spiritual ministry. With spiritual discernment you are able to minister to your brothers and sisters because you know what they need. You know where they are. You are not deceived by outward appearance. You touch people's spirit. You sense what is within and you are able to help when other people are not able to. That is the use of spiritual discernment. So seek spiritual discernment. But remember, always seek it in love and in humility.

Shall we pray:

Lord, there is something that Thou dost desire to give to Thy people, something needed, desperately needed, important to us and to the maturity of the church. Lord, we do pray that if it is Thy will, then we want it, but we want it for Thee and not for ourselves. Oh, keep us always in humility and in love. We ask in Thy precious name. Amen.

Other Books Printed By
Christian Testimony Ministry

Speaker	Title
Dana Congdon	Marriage, Singleness, and the Will of God
	Recovery & Restoration
	The Holy Spirit
	Hebrews
A.J. Flack	Tent of His Splendour
Stephen Kaung	Acts
	Be Ye Therefore Perfect
	Called Out Unto Christ
	Called to the Fellowship of God's Son
	Divine Life and Order
	For Me to Live is Christ
	Glorious Liberty of the Children of God
	God's Purpose for the Family
	I Will Build My Church
	Meditations on the Kingdom
	Recovery
	Spiritual Exercise
	Spiritual Life (II Corinthians Series)
	Teach Us to Pray
	The Cross
	The Fulness of Christ—In the Book of Revelation
	The Headship of Christ
	The Kingdom and the Church
	The Kingdom of God
	The Last Call to the Churches, the Call to Overcome
	The Life of Our Lord Jesus
	The Life of the Church, the Body of Christ
	The Lord's Table
	Two Guideposts for Inheriting the Kingdom
	Vision of Christ (Revelation)
	Who Are We?

WHY DO WE SO GATHER?
WORSHIP

LANCE LAMBERT   CALLED UNTO HIS ETERNAL GLORY
                    GOD'S ETERNAL PURPOSE
                    IN THE DAY OF THY POWER
                    JACOB I HAVE LOVED
                    LIVING FAITH
                    LESSONS FROM THE LIFE OF MOSES
                    LOVE DIVINE
                    MY HOUSE SHALL BE A HOUSE OF PRAYER
                    PREPARATION FOR THE COMING OF THE LORD
                    REIGNING WITH CHRIST
                    SPIRITUAL CHARACTER
                    THE GOSPEL OF THE KINGDOM
                    THE IMPORTANCE OF COVERING
                    THE LAST DAYS AND GOD'S PRIORITIES
                    THE PRIZE
                    THE SUPREMACY OF JESUS CHRIST
                    THINE IS THE POWER!
                    THOU ART MINE

T. AUSTIN-SPARKS   THE LORD'S TESTIMONY AND THE WORLD NEED

HARVEY CEDARS CONFERENCE

STEPHEN KAUNG   HEAVENLY VISION
                     SPIRITUAL RESPONSIBILITY

CONGDON, HILE, KAUNG   SPIRITUAL MINISTRY
                         SPIRITUAL AUTHORITY
                         SPIRITUAL HOUSE
                         SPIRITUAL SUBMISSION

STEPHEN KAUNG   SPIRITUAL KNOWLEDGE
                     SPIRITUAL POWER
                     SPIRITUAL REALITY
                     SPIRITUAL VALUE
                     SPIRITUAL BLESSING
                     SPIRITUAL DISCERNMENT

www.ingramcontent.com/pod-product-compliance
Lightning Source LLC
Chambersburg PA
CBHW060721030426
42337CB00017B/2949